PLACE IN RETURN BOX to remove this checkout from your record.
TO AVOID FINES return on or before date due.

DATE DUE	DATE DUE	DATE DUE
————	————	————
————	————	————
————	————	————
————	————	————
————	————	————
————	————	————
————	————	————

Post-Cold War Peace and Securi Prospects in Southern Africa

Severine Rugumamu

Occasional Paper Series No. 5

Post-Cold War Peace and Security Prospects in Southern Africa

Severine Rugumamu

Post-Cold War Peace and Security Prospects in Southern Africa

SAPES BOOKS
HARARE

First published 1993
by SAPES Books
P.O. Box MP 111
Mount Pleasant
Harare
Zimbabwe

Typeset by Southern Africa Printing & Publishing House (SAPPHO) (Pvt) Ltd,
95 Harare Street, Harare, Zimbabwe

Cover design by Hassan Musa

Printed by Strand Multiprint, Harare, Zimbabwe

ISBN 1-77905-010-0

Contents

Contents

Post-Cold War Peace and Security Prospects in Southern Africa*

1. Introduction

One of the primary roles of the state is to provide peace and security for its citizens both within the nation-state and to ensure their protection against threats from outside. This function has always been considered vital for purposes of enabling the citizens to conduct their social lives in harmony and unencumbered. To perform this function effectively, the state has, on the one hand, to command a critical mass of institutional capabilities to regulate societal relations, extract resources, and provide the standard "public goods" of which peace and security are primary.[1] On the other, it needs widespread mass support and loyalty. As the histories of developed European states amply demonstrate, the above capabilities were developed and nurtured through long periods of protracted social struggles, battles and wars.

It is argued in this paper that sustainable peace and security in the Southern African sub-region has, for a long time, been elusive. The region inherited from colonialism a virtually conflict-prone environment. This included, among other things, distorted and dependent economic structures, incoherent social compositions, a legacy of fragile institutions and big power interventions. Given those trying circumstances, the paper further argues, weak post-independence regimes understandably paid inordinate attention to the questions of survival rather than to the broad issues of societal integration, political participation or to economic restructuring. The end of the Cold War, therefore, does not, in our view, promise any brighter prospects for peace and security in this sub-region. The future seems to be overshadowed by dark prospects of even much more protracted violent conflicts. Nor is the definite course of the unfolding political processes nationally, regionally and internationally easily predictable in the wake of an emerging unipolar political and military world; of regional economic restructuring and rehabilitation of war devastated economies; resettling millions of refugees, returning exiles and demobilized soldiers; nationally managing the ensuing competitive politics; and, containing the possible reassertion of the Republic of South Africa as the regional hegemon.

In the conventional international relations literature, definitions of national security were not only nebulous and ambiguous, but also often value loaded. However, what was common to all definitions, was the fact that they were curiously dependent on one variable . . . threat perceptions. The most intriguing part of it all, however, has always been how to specify the referent objects of peace and security. Whose peace and whose security? Is it that of a nation-state, of a social class, of a specific nationality in a nation-state, or simply that of a regime in power? The second equally important question is security from what kinds of threats? Is it from external aggression; domestic turmoil; spillover of instabilities from adjacent territory or from environmental destruction? Or is it simply insecurity paranoia? Finally and most important, who defines the threat? Is it by elected government officials or by a self-imposed regime? Is it by an internally suppressed nationality or by an exploited social class? It bears remembering at this early stage that perceptions in politics, whether real or imaginary, are infinitely more important than the reality itself. Political perceptions dictate behaviour and, in fact, reality would weigh much less than beliefs, myths or obsessions (Hoffmann, 1980:10).

The purpose of this paper is three-fold. First, it defines and critiques the mainstream western scholarship on national security as it relates to threat perceptions and management in the Third World. Secondly, it attempts to elaborate on a theoretical framework within which threat perceptions in the African countries should be studied and explained. Thirdly and finally, the proposed framework is applied to examine peace and security prospects in the Southern African sub-region in the post-cold war era.

2. National Security Theories: An Overview

Wolfers (1962) and Bukan (1966) conceded that the term security *per se* was an "ambiguous symbol" with many meanings. Different security levels of analysis . . . national, international and global[2] . . . refer to different sets of issues and are, in turn, each based on different theoretical and political assumptions that are closely linked to the historical evolution of the international system and the intellectual progress in its interpretation. Each of those levels of analysis has at least three clusters of interpretations namely, the realist and idealist based on different theoretical assumptions about the nature of man and the behaviour of states. The third cluster of interpretation often seeks to bridge the gap between the two interpretations by developing converging concepts, building on the ability of man and the state for rational behaviour (Haftendorn, 1991:5-6).

The pre-occupation with peace and security is as old as human society itself. At a national level, however, security concerns emerged in a specific historical setting. With the birth of the nation-state in the 17th century, and its interest in national survival, national security became a prominent concern. To end the Hobbesian ''war of all against all'', the sovereign was entrusted with securing domestic peace and safeguarding the life and property of the people against any foreign threats (Hobbes, 1957). Diplomacy and war became the prime means to further national causes.

The traditional realist research approaches as initially developed and applied by American political scientists to study national security were couched exclusively in military-strategic terms.[3] Realism achieved its intellectual prominence in the post-World War II theorizing about international relations in the US and spread to Europe and much later to the Third World. The theory was based on two assumptions. The first assumption was that threats to the state security arose from outside its borders. The apparent domestic sources of insecurity in the United Kingdom over Northern Island, Spain over the Basques or Canada over Quebec were brushed aside as exceptions that confirmed the rule. The second assumption was that those threats were primarily, if not exclusively, military in nature. Security studies of the day examined threats, use, control of military force and diplomacy. Berkowitz and Bock (1968) defined national security as ''the ability of a nation-state to protect its internal core values from external threats''. The core values that were traditionally cited for protection included, protection of territorial integrity, preservation of national sovereignty, and the survival of individuals within the nation-state.

Over time, however, the theoretical parameters of the traditional realist framework were redefined and broadened (Koehen and Nye, 1976). It was increasingly realized that the security of one state was closely linked to that of other states. Herz's (1950) ''security dilemma'' thesis . . . that an increase in one state's security decreased the security of others . . . came to the fore once again. In Kenneth Waltz's words (1979:64) ''the means of security for one state are, in their very existence, the means by which other states are threatened''. At the theoretical level, the importance of international security concerns replaced those at the national level, and so also was the singularity of military threats by wider definitions of security. Moreover, those neo-realist theoretical redefinitions were further informed by relatively new actors in international politics. Besides states, non-state actors such as transnational corporations, terrorist groups, multilateral organizations and the like were added. Additionally, the range of issues that came to fall under the rubric of national security were also broadened to include, among other things, the protection of the international market economy, ideology, and pretty recently, the environment, drugs and AIDS . . . once again from external enemies. Those who included the economic issues in the national security equation, for instance, tended to concentrate largely on the security of strategically high-ranked resources and the economic functions of war systems located outside the nation-state (Krause and Nye, 1975). That reformulation was succinctly put forward by Nye (1990:157) that:

> With changing actors in world politics come changing goals. In the traditional view, the state gave priority to military security to ensure their survival. Today, however, states must consider new dimensions of security. National security has become more complicated as threats shift from the military (that is, threats to territorial integrity) to the economic and ecological.

By logical extension, the management of national security was traditionally framed around two distinct, but closely related variables: the security environment and the readiness of the hardware. The former referred to the nature of the external threats and alliance patterns, and the latter to the physical capabilities and the tangible policy infrastructure comprising of strategic doctrine, force structure, intelligence and weapon choice. Thus, for a realist, national security could be maintained by an accumulation of coercive power or by entering into security alliances or both. The centrality of the military power, however, took precedence over security alliances. Logically, and as a result, national security waxes or wanes with the ability of the state to deter an attack or to defeat it. Lippmann's (1943:51) much quoted advice underscores this truism:

> . . . a nation is secure to the extent to which it is not in danger of having to sacrifice core values if it wishes to avoid the war, and it is able if challenged to maintain them by victory in such a war.

In the 1960s, with the Cuban missile crisis as a catalyst, it was increasingly realized that, in fact, security is indivisible. With the increased complexity of interdependence and the high level of technological development, the security of nations, peoples and individuals could not be separated from that of others (Hjelm-Wallen, 1991:25). The concept of international security implied that the security of one state was closely linked to that of other states. In short, states were interdependent in the security affairs such that the security of one is strongly affected by the actions of others and vice versa. That realization brought to the fore the need for security regimes among states which shared common external threats and enemies.[4] For that had been a practice since the end of World War II. The structure of the international system had consisted of a combination of alliance networks and a system of nuclear deterrence. The former regulated more cooperative endeavour, and the latter more confrontational relationship.

The rationale for this external orientation among developed western countries is not far to seek. In the first place, when the theory was being developed, the process of state formation and national consolidation in most Western countries had long been a reality. The components of the state, that is, the idea of the state, its institutional expression and its physical base, were accepted as legitimate both domestically and internationally. Moreover, the domestic institutions of governance had established conditions and traditions for long-term stability and predictability. In other words, the state authority was assumed to command broad-based legitimacy. Precisely because the degree of internal vulnerability was assumed to be low, realists were legitimately justified to focus their intellectual concerns exclusively on the external environment to ensure that it was favourable for the survival of the core values of the state; and for superpowers that had then emerged, it was necessary for them to ensure the extension of their national values on a global scale (Osgood,1981:2).

2.1 Inadequacies of Realism

Realist approaches have often been used for example, to compare "power politics" and "nuclear paralysis" theories that seek to explain which states are the most responsible for the overall frequency of foreign overt military intervention and the geographic scope of international armed conflicts in the nuclear age (Tillema,1989; Bull, 1984). Without going into the explanations for each war, such studies often concluded that great powers resort to military force infrequently compared to aggressive minor states. Intuitively, therefore, Third World states were perceived as the main source of threats to the international peace and security which was organized on a bipolar collective security arrangement.

Korany (1989), Ayoob, (1991) Nyong'o (1986) have written disparagingly on the crudity of this framework as applied to the Third World national security environments by arguing that it has resulted in ethnocentrism, flawed in explanation, a misconceived theory that has neglected the specificities of the Third World state formation and the types of conflicts prevalent in these societies: intra-state or domestic conflicts. Besides pervasive external meddling in internal affairs, many nation-states in the Third World suffer from economic underdevelopment, unstable political systems, ethnic and other social cleavages that are permanent threats to peace and security. To simply focus on external threats as realists used to believe, is to miss the whole point.

From a Third World vantage point, the mainstream realist approaches to national security suffer from at least four fundamental flaws. In the first place, the emphasis on the accumulation, maintenance and development of a military force has been found to be no panacea for Africa's complex security problems. To be sure, military strength is a necessary but not sufficient guardian. The national security anchored on mere military build-up in predominantly structurally weak and dependent economies has had very severe limitations. As the recent historical experiences of Mozambique, Angola, Zaire and Ethiopia have evidently shown, the obsession with accumulation of military power by the ruling regimes entailed extensive trade-offs with their domestic social and economic priorities, which in the long run, undermined their overall national security postures (Kemp, 1977; Arlinghaus, 1983; Ross, 1988). Not infrequently also, the accumulated military strength in a variety of African states has been used by the ruling regimes to consolidate their political power by suppressing their political rivals. The Mengistu of Ethiopia and the Mobutu of Zaire have deployed the national security instruments to suppress genuine opposition in the name of the national interest. In other words, what passes for national security in most parts of Africa is basically regime security. As was argued above, the multiple vulnerabilities of African states compel us to look at the deeper structure and the boarder spectrum of issues than what the received realist wisdom is capable of offering (Azar and Moon, 1988:11).

The second flaw built in the realist approaches in the study of national security in the Third World is the skewed conceptualization of the "security environment." In the conventional international relations literature, this subject refers to the external threat and alliance patterns. In the bi-polar security alliances of post-World War II period, the institutional security structures were basically tied to ideological affinity as well as to geo-political calculations. The nature of Africa's external threats and the kinds of alliance arrangements that evolved were, to say the least, completely different from those envisaged by the western establishments. The internal and external sources of threats are inextricably linked in Africa. Any attempts at the demarcation between the two is considered fruitless. Africa's major external threats include, among others, those arising from disputed colonial boundaries, transnational corporations, and those from irredentist tendencies. In this regard, therefore, Africa's external and internal sources of insecurity are so inextricably interlinked that it is ridiculous to disentangle them (Rugumamu, 1991a). Granted this reasoning alone, the African conditions should prove strangely irrelevant for this framework. The third problem associated with the realist approaches is the question of legitimacy. As already noted, the state authority in most Western nation-states enjoys broad-based legitimacy from its citizenry. This is so precisely because the rules of political competition, participation and governance have long been settled. Those who, through the accepted rules and procedures, ultimately capture state power have, in theory, the nation's mandate to rule. It is that kind of state legitimacy that determines, to a large extent, the national will, morale and the character of its citizens. A broad-based state legitimacy excludes almost invariably, massive challenges to the exercise of its authority (Morgenthau, 1948).

Unlike in those Western liberal democracies, however, African states suffer from acute legitimacy crisis which severely constrain their security performance. The structural political rigidities, economic under-development and scarcity of resources seldom allow these governments to enjoy the functional competence and legal appropriateness which are essential to the creation and maintenance of legitimacy. Moreover, the endemic failure of governments to meet the basic needs of their citizens, regular suppression of the people's demands for participation, jobs and justice are both determinants and resultants of this crisis of legitimacy. Above all, the irregular political changes (themselves consequences of limited political participation) such as military coups, palace coups along with arbitrary and autocratic rule, deepen Africa's legitimacy crisis and, in turn, exacerbates the national security posture of these countries (Jackson and Rosberg, 1983; 1982; MacFarlane, 1984;).

The faltering legitimacy in many African countries and the erosion of political authority combine to increase the internal and external threats and vulnerabilities to the regime in power. This usually takes the form of political protests, sabotages, revolts and rebellions. As the regime in power tries to respond to and control these threats in the name of "national security", it destroys the national security *per se*. Such insecurity environment was further compounded during the Cold War period where the contending faction, just like the state itself, was also externally supported. All the above clearly reveals that the complexity of the security environment in the Third World could not be easily and fruitfully explained by the realist framework.

The last shortcoming associated with realist approaches to national security in the Third World is the issue of integration. The received conventional theory of conceptualizing and analyzing national security assumed a unitary nation-state with commonly shared national values. In Africa, however, about a century ago, colonialism lumped together inveterate ethnic, religiouş, and racial groups in one territorial entity. These nationalities were expected, over time, to evolve into one composite nation-state with commonly shared national values and to evolve commonly agreed political rules and regulations. Unfortunately that dream has turned into a nightmare. African nation-states continue to comprise of numerous, fragmented and competing nationalities that pose a security problem to the state, peoples and individuals. Genuine "nationalist" efforts to assimilate, accommodate or even contain politically dissatisfied nationalities, continue to be greeted with violent reactions from a whole range of societal cleavages (Horowitz, 1981). In this sense, therefore, the very idea of a state in Africa still lacks the broad societal consensus and mobilizing ideologies. As a result, the physical base of the state, its organizing ideologies and legitimacy continue to be vigorously contested in whatever corner of the continent one wishes to turn.

2.2 What are Security Issues in Africa?

In the recent past, and especially because of the opportunities engendered by the demise of the Cold War, dissolution of the former Soviet Union and the retreat of the socialist ideology, a redefinition of security has been necessitated. There have been various attempts to broaden the concept of security so as to incorporate not only the traditional realist contents of the "overt", but also the "covert" ones. Thus, issues such as poverty, disease, environmental degradation, drugs, human rights violation and most importantly, lack of democracy, have come to be directly linked to the concept of security. Indeed, the beauty of this multi-dimensional approach is that it considers most of the relevant social, economic, political, military and even cultural issues as a package (Holsti, 1992; Arnold, 1991; The Kampala Document, 1991).[5]

Much as the above so-called multi-dimensional approach seeks to be all inclusive, it is basically ahistorical. It simply attempts to work with only the contemporary realities and ignores completely their history. It is the contention of this paper that in order to study meaningfully peace and security in Africa, it is imperative to analyze the implications of both its past history and the consequent contemporary reality (Mandaza, 1991). The role played by imperialism in the creation of conflict-prone environment on the continent during the colonial period constitute, in our opinion, the historical basis for the present insecurity patterns. The arbitrary creation of nation-states, the colonial legacy of divide and rule, and the incorporation of Africa into the iniquitous global capitalist economic system, should serve as the logical starting point. The failure to appreciate the critical role of colonial history leads some analysts into all kinds of bourgeois stereotypes. How else does one explain pervasive boundary conflicts on the continent? What business does the IMF have in sovereign African states? Finally, are reserves and homelands in the Southern African sub-region the African natural habitats? These and other similar questions can hardly be answered without a recourse to history. They are, in our view, some of the major causes of insecurity in the region.

Secondly, and equally important, is the exclusion of the whole question of the Cold War in the current theorization attempts about peace and security in Africa. Much too often, those attempts are obsessed with celebrating the end of the Cold War and assuming away its continued legacy in the perceptions of the people in the region. To be sure, the parameters of peace and security in Africa were defined primarily by a complex pattern of superpower conflict and competition for ideological, economic and military hegemony on a global scale. Each superpower zealously believed that it was only by increasing its power and influence in any region of the world that peace and stability could be promoted and sustained. Understandably, during that whole period, Africa's peace and security rose and fell as a function of the temporal importance that was attached to it by the superpowers. Old legacies die hard. The conflicts that were sowed by the Cold War, just like those by colonialism, are here to stay for quite some time. To assume the Cold War is behind us once and for all, is simply to miss the point. How else does one explain the continued civil war in Angola and Mozambique?

Thirdly, any serious attempt at analyzing the insecurity environment in the region, should strive to link the "weak state",[6] to its nascent democratic traditions and practices (if any), irredentist and secessionist tendencies among minorities, boundary disputes and so on in order to serve as guiding posts through the maze of the region's sources of insecurity. In this sense, then, any proposals aimed at national consolidation, confidence and security building mechanisms, regional cooperation and integration, should never lose sight of those significant historical issues. In the following section we apply this framework to explain peace and security in the Southern African sub-region.

3. Colonial Heritage and Southern Africa's Insecurity

Many a time, the European colonization of the African continent is deservedly blamed for the arbitrary "balkanization" of the continent into unviable economic and political entities.[7] Rarely, however, does colonialism receive a similar fitting blame for the post-colonial boundaries problems. Herbst (1989) observed that the arbitrarily drawn African political boundaries were based either on colonial administrative convenience or on intra-imperial trade-offs. Describing the arbitrary nature of the partition process of the continent by European powers, Lord Salisbury then British Secretary of State for Colonies refreshingly noted:

> . . . (we) have been engaged in drawing lines upon maps where no white man's foot ever trod; we have been giving away mountains and rivers and lakes to each other, only hindered by the small impediment that we never knew exactly where the mountains and rivers and lakes were" (quoted in Ajala, 19831:180).

The colonial ignorance about the continent that they were dividing among themselves, coupled with the colonizer contempt for the colonized, explains largely why about 44 percent of those boundaries are geometrical, mainly in straight lines that either correspond to an astrologic measurement or are parallel to some other set of lines (Sautter, 1982:42). This unfortunate legacy of boundaries has left an indelible mark on the evolution of the continent's political development. They have turned out to be one of the major sources of insecurity on the continent. As Lord Curzon (1907:7) correctly observed, boundaries are a razor's edge on which hang suspended the modern issues of war and peace, of life or death to nations, and just as the protection of the home is the most vital of the private citizen, so the integrity of her borders is the condition of existence of the state.

Those arbitrary borders were drawn without respect for social, historical, demographic or linguistic groupings criteria. What is even worse, both the colonial and post-colonial political authorities charged with maintaining them have been too weak. It is also partly, but largely because of the latter's structural weaknesses that led to the inclusion of Article 3 of the Charter establishing the Organization of African Unity (OAU) in 1964 calling on all member states "to affirm sovereign equality of all member states, non-interference in the internal affairs of member states, and respect for their sovereignty and territorial integrity".

Moreover, the international community in the post-World War II era greatly elevated the norm of sovereignty (Jackson, 1990). It allowed any country no matter how underdeveloped its political and economic institutions were, to enjoy the full privileges of sovereignty. At the same time, it was considered a violation of a country's sovereignty if the world community supported a dissident ethnic group which was dissatisfied with its government in power. Moreover, the Cold War conditions provided weak African states with the necessary protection when their fragile sovereignties were threatened. Zaire won crucial support from the US government to quell the Shaba secessionist group. Mengistu's Ethiopia was provided with the critical military support by the Soviets to repel Somalia's irredentist claims and to contain several secessionist groups.

The colonial expansion in the Southern African sub-region divided the vast region in separate mini-economies: the extensive semi-desert of Botswana and Namibia, and the mountainous outcroppings of Lesotho and Swaziland, are occupied by a half to a little more than a million inhabitants each. The landlocked Malawi, Zambia, and Zimbabwe each has a population of somewhat more than five million situated on more fertile lands and including variable agricultural and mineral resources. Finally, are much larger oddly shaped coastal states of Mozambique and Angola with populations of less than ten million. In the Republic of South Africa, the Group Areas Act delineated the areas to be occupied by various races. The said Act denied majority control over the rich resources of their homeland. The Land Apportionment Act of 1930 in colonial Zimbabwe also excluded Africans from permanent rights to land in the so-called European areas and reserved less than half of the colony's land for Africans. The reserved rich lands were offered to giant foreign mining and farming corporations and white settlers for farming and mining. At the same time, colonial governments forcefully resettled African peasants in the overcrowded, infertile Tribal Trust Lands (Seidman, 1985:13). The land question in this sub-region was one of the root causes of insecurity during the colonial period and it so is in the post-colonial era.

The African boundaries are permeable and so frequently permeated. A number of African states and nationalist groups have, since independence, challenged the legitimacy of the inherited boundaries and the resultant territorial apportionments. Boundary disputes have given rise to the never-ending irredentist and secessionist politics on the continent. Attempts to secure the return of the "lost lands" or to secede from colonially apportioned territories have involved the use of warfare, subversion, severance of relations as well as big power interventions. Contrary to the much publicized literature on the causes of insecurity in Africa, Zartman (1966:105-112) aptly concluded over two decades ago that the problems created by colonial boundaries are among the more frequent causes of war in Africa. However, to imply by the sheer frequency of wars, as some realists do, that Africans are more bellicose than others, is nothing but intellectual dishonesty that borders on racism.

Tanzania has had border disputes with Malawi as well as with Uganda. As a retaliation against Tanzania's continued support for Malawi political dissidents, President Banda announced in 1968 that, by right, some 1,000 square miles of Tanzanian land on the borders of Lake Nyasa belonged to Malawi. This unilateral provocation led to the deterioration of relations between the two nations and a mutual suspicion (Nelson *et al.* 1975: 186-187). Ten years later, General Amin of Uganda challenged the colonial boundaries of the two countries. He argued that he could only recognize the natural borders between the two countries. He went ahead and physically occupied the Kagera River salient on the Tanzanian side "in order to seek a natural boundary of security along the river." It was about one hundred square miles of the Tanzanian territory. This resulted in a bitter war between the two countries and an eventual overthrow of the General from power.

Another boundary dispute is between Namibia and South Africa. Recently the Republic of South Africa has impudently refused to hand over the Walvis Bay territory and twelve off-shore Penguine islands to Namibia. This has been done in contravention of the United Nations Security Council Resolution 432 of 1978 which recognized both the bay and the islands as part and parcel of Namibia. This intransigence on the part of South Africa will continue to be one of the sources of tension and insecurity between the two neighbouring states.

Much more recent were the border tensions between Namibia and Botswana over the territorial ownership of an uninhabited Sidudu (Kisikili) Island, located in the Chobe River around March 1992. As Maluwa (1992:18-22) has ably demonstrated, the latest disputes over the Sidudu Islands has its roots in the colonial arrangements embodied in the Anglo-German Agreement of July 1 1890. That Agreement has been subjected to different interpretations ever since it was written, not only by the colonizing powers themselves, but also by the local inhabitants. The problem in the present dispute, just as before, essentially centres around the proper identification of which of the several channels constitutes "the main channel of the river" which marked the boundary. The incident was followed by a brief deployment of troops and the erection of military positions in the area by both countries before diplomatic efforts were deployed to cool down the tensions. We have every reason to believe that the recent round of disputes between the two otherwise friendly governments over the same island is not the last one.

Besides the question of borders, there is the whole question of effectively managing the inherited western political institutions. Ibingira (1980:1-59) legitimately charged that having completely marginalized African political institutions, colonialism provided inadequate preparations to Africans in managing alien institutions that they had imposed on them . . . institutions that are not grounded in African political traditions. As Tilly (1975) and Cohen *et al.* (1981) graphically demonstrated, it took Europe three to four centuries to build differentiated, autonomous, centralized organizations. In our view, it would be simply naive to expect African societies to internalize foreign imposed institutions in a matter of only three decades. This, however, should be no excuse for outright misuse of power by African rulers. One African state after another have failed, out of sheer self interest, to establish a socio-political environment in which legitimate demands of individuals or groups could be satisfactorily addressed, and in which conflicts of interests could be peacefully resolved. To be sure, a sustained conducive socio-political environment has to prevail in order to ensure that these traditions and practices are developed and nurtured so as to be part and parcel of a nation's culture. Once again, one of the sources of insecurity in Africa has not only been the inability on the part of local leaders to fully internalize inherited political and social institutions in the last three or so decades, but also the failure to do so, at times, served their narrow vested interests.

The colonial legacy of divide-and-rule sowed its own seeds of insecurity for the post-colonial nation building in Africa. As if the lumping together of heterogeneous ethnic, religious and racial communities were not enough, the colonialists resorted to a divide-and-rule policy which sought to play on and strengthen historical differences among those communities in order to pre-empt a unified anti-colonial force. In the Southern African sub-region the Tribal Trust Land and the Group Areas Acts facilitated to consolidate such divisive sentiments among Africans. Besides the institution of central government, colonialism created semi-autonomous local governments and civil societies based on ethnic, racial, religious or regional considerations. To further enrich those parochial sentiments, the colonial governments approved and often supported nationalist movements and civil associations centred around those narrow social bases. As majority rule approached in Zimbabwe, for example, the two deeply divided ethnic factions ended up forming competing political parties. The division has continued to widen long after independence. The Buganda

Kingdom in Uganda is another example. It was made to consider itself as a separate nation within colonial Uganda. Surprisingly, such divisive practices were even written into independence constitutions for Nigeria, Uganda and recently for Zimbabwe giving special concessions for specific sections of society. Some genuine nationalist efforts in the post-colonial period designed to uproot those divisive tendencies have often degenerated into unprecedented security crises in several African countries.

That was not all. The colonial system went further to economically exploit and politically oppress each social category separately. Nyong'o's (1986:576-78) characterization of colonialism as "a structure of violence" clearly captures its apartheid variant in South Africa. Apartheid as a system of political oppression, economic exploitation and ideological degradation has dehumanized the African man, deprived him of his birth rights, exploited his labour and resources for the development of the settler class. This racially organized exploitation has naturally generated significant prosperity for the minority white society and explosive social pressures from all other races. Apartheid systematically and inequitably discriminates between races in terms of human fundamentals: access to education, employment, housing, the dignities of family life, the enjoyment of civil and political life.

To maintain that *status quo*, the apartheid system has constantly resorted to the use of brutal force and repression not only against its disgruntled majority citizens but also against the neighbouring sovereign African states of Zambia, Zimbabwe, Mozambique, Angola and Botswana that provided the sanctuary to the nationalist military wings as well as apartheid refugees. The political economy of apartheid and South Africa's destabilization campaigns are so well known that their repetition would be superfluous (Goldsworth, 1980; Davies *et al.* 1979). Suffice only to indicate a few statistics that ably demonstrate the degree of violence and destruction that Apartheid has inflicted on the sub-region:

> Since 1980, the South African state violence against its neighbouring states has resulted in a minimum of 1.6 million lives being lost, more than 11 million people largely women and children being made homeless, over 750,000 children being orphaned, abandoned or otherwise traumatized, and at least US$60 billion in war damage to precious schools, hospitals, bridges, highways and development projects (UNICEF, 1989:1925).

Additionally, South Africa's aggression has meant that the Front Line States of Mozambique, Angola, Zambia, Botswana, Zimbabwe and

Tanzania had to channel millions of dollars into defence needs instead of developing more and better education, health, water and food systems. For most of the 1980s, the Angolan and Mozambican governments were spending well over fifty percent of their national revenues on national security alone.

From this short historical detour, it is definitely plausible to argue that the genesis of insecurity in the Southern African sub-region today, like elsewhere on the continent, is unmistakably colonialism. Its rich mineral resources endowment, the geostrategic location of the Cape of Good Hope and the Indian Ocean, later elevated the strategic significance of this region in the East-West security calculations. The physical presence of the two superpowers only helped to escalate domestic conflicts in Mozambique, Angola and Zimbabwe. This meant the acquisition of better and more lethal war machine as well as foreign military advisors. As was argued elsewhere (Rugumamu, 1991b), the two superpowers exploited the domestic and regional weaknesses and conflicts of the continent often for reasons not directly related to the conflicts themselves.

Finally comes the issue of economics. The causal relationship between colonialism and the current Africa's economic dependence and underdevelopment is rarely challenged (Rodney, 1982). Indeed, colonialism restructured African economies in such a way as to complement those of Europe. From then onwards the continent's economic fortunes were umbilically tied to what happened in Europe. The structure of production, investment and trade were largely determined by the economic imperatives of the metropolitan economies. Those economic structures have remained unaltered even after twenty-some years of political independence. In the post-independence era, however, the International Monetary Fund, the World Bank, and the Paris and London Clubs of creditors have increasingly come to define and police over the basic macroeconomic policies of the former colonies. The consortium of Bankers has assumed the role of former colonial powers and is widely perceived as the instrument of domination in the world capitalist system (Payer, 1974).

As a result of persistent economic crises of the 1970s and 1980s (crises of the capitalist system itself), coupled with a widespread, severe and persistent drought, that consortium of bankers now wields unprecedented power in Africa. The sheer acceptance of the IMF policy packages, often times a reversal of national policies, is an encroachment on the very sovereignty of these states . . . one of the basic core values in the realist national security tradition. The rigid debt rescheduling and balance of payments support loan conditions have often provoked political insecurity in Africa (Girvan, 1980; Loxley, 1987). Violent street riots and military coups have been reported in Egypt (1977), Sudan (1982, 1985), Morocco (1984), Tunisia (1983, 1984), Zambia (1990) and in Nigeria (1983, 1985). Thus, the root causes of Africa's economic insecurity, like those in the realm of politics, have their origins in colonialism. Their permanent solutions have to be sought in the destruction of those colonial structures that give rise to this pattern of insecurity. We shall come to this point later.

3.1 Superpower Rivalry and Africa's Security

As was earlier pointed out, with the rise of the two superpowers after World War II, their national security concerns assumed a global rather than a traditional national dimension. This was facilitated by the broad power equilibrium that had been established as a result of mutually tolerated progressive consolidation of a bipolar two-bloc alliance structure of the Warsaw Pact and NATO (Osgood, 1981:2). With these new developments, the neo-realist came to redefine the national security of the superpowers and big powers as "that part of government policy having as its objective the creation of national and international political conditions favourable to the protection or extension of vital values against existing and potential adversaries" (Trager and Kronenberg, 1973:4). It is against this definitional reformulation and refinement, that the security of all other nation-states inevitably entered, in one way or another, into the security calculations of the two superpowers. In this sense, therefore, the security of any African nation-state was no more than its relative importance to the global strategic interests of the superpowers. Africa's security as an independent unit of analysis assumed limited explanatory value. This is yet another dimension that makes the received theory incapable of capturing the entire security dynamics of the African environment.

At the height of the Cold War conflict in the 1950s and 1960s, the superpower perceptions of each other took on a Manichean image of a world divided between the forces of good and evil. This mutual suspicion and rivalry continued into the detente period. This was exemplified by *The 1988 US National Security Strategy* which categorically portrayed this paranoid outlook that:

> The most significant threat to the United States security interests remains the global challenge posed by the Soviet Union . . . The Soviet Union places high priority on creating and exploiting divisions within and among the Western allies. In key developing countries it supports communists that seek to undermine

governments allied with or friendly to the United States and to replace them with the authoritarian or totalitarian regimes (1988:5).

In the same vein, the Moscow establishment perceived Washington as the primary "source of world evil". The late Marshall Grechkov (1975), then Minister of Defence of the Soviet Union, saw the principal threat to the Soviet national security as the imperialist world led by the United States. He explained:

At the present stage, the historical function of the Soviet Armed Forces is not restricted merely to their function in defending our motherland and other socialist countries, the Soviet state actively and purposely opposes the export of counter-revolution and the policy of oppression, supports the national liberation struggles and resolutely resists imperialist aggression in whatever distant region of our planet it may appear.

In a race to win new allies, maintain old ones or secure additional military bases in Africa and elsewhere, superpowers passionately sought to participate directly or indirectly through their surrogates, in the domestic and regional politics. As we shall have occasion to argue, the superpower involvement in African politics revived and even escalated the conflicts that were sowed by colonialism a century earlier. In the following pages, we explore the superpower interests in the continent, how they were pursued, and, in turn, how that impacted on Africa's security environment.

The national security planners of both superpowers had long realized Africa's geostrategic importance in their global power competition. In particular, the strategic importance of Africa's coasts proved an irresistible lure. The Maghreb constitutes a bridge linking Africa to Europe. The Mediterranean is the intersection between east-west and north-south axis. Northeastern Africa links the continent to the Middle East and the Indian Ocean. Southern Africa is a major commercial and navy waterway around the Cape of Good Hope to Europe and the Americas (Jouve, 1985 :306-308). For these reasons, the Americans and Soviets massively developed their power projection capabilities in and around the continent. On America's strategic interests in the continent, Tarabrin (1983:46-47), argued that Africa was just one of its many strategic points in its integrated global security network:

. . . they view the African continent as one of the basic components of a system of "forward lines" along which "possibilities" for defending the zones of vital interests of the USA" must be created and defended. Leaning on this imperial conception, Washington has begun to build military presence in Africa. Emphasis is placed upon nations occupying a geographical position which is convenient from a military strategic point of view, possessing viable ports, airfields and other components of military infrastructure, and also disposing significant natural resources.

Irrespective of what the former Soviet officialdom publicly claimed to have been its African foreign policy, we are convinced that in its security calculations, it sought to reduce the American and Western influence, minimize Communist China's impact, and above all, obtain military bases and other facilities in order to improve its overall power projection capability (Donaldson, 1981; Albright, 1973; Vorobyev,1978). As earlier pointed out, Africa's fragile political regimes, often backed up by limited domestic support and resources, craved for superpower sponsorship to remain in power. They offered their airbases, harbours and even their deserts for bases. As *quid pro quo*, African leaders got not only weapons and military advisors, but also assured protection from all kinds of threats.[8] And those who succeeded in entering into security alliances with either of them discovered eventually how fast they had to compromise their highly cherished autonomy and independence and how quickly they were alienated internally. In retrospect, the Machiavellian dictum that "a prince ought never make a common cause with one more powerful than himself" should be as instructive to African governments today as it was then in discouraging unequal alliances.

The problems of Africa's security have been further compounded by the superpowers and big powers arms transfers. The United States and the former Soviet Union, for example, consistently used arms transfer to the Third World in general and to Africa in particular as their principal foreign policy instrument (Ottaway, 1984:165-194). Ideological friends were won and sustained by a constant supply of weapons. As cases of Ethiopia and Somalia amply demonstrated, both superpowers at different times used arms transfer not only as partial payment for their military bases and visiting rights, but also as a means of winning, maintaining and propping up their political allies in Africa. It is important to emphasize once again that military build-ups in Africa have not helped to increase the national security posture as the realist theory would have liked us believe, but did the opposite instead. More and more weapon transfers to Africa brought in its trails greater human carnage and untold destruction of property.

The compulsion of each superpower to intervene in crisis situations in order to preclude the other, went a long way to internationalize Africa's domestic conflicts. The list of such interventions is long. A few examples are in order. The last three successive American governments backed the Moroccan government's claims to the former Spanish colony of Western Sahara, largely because the nationalist movement of Polisario was receiving military support from the former communist countries. In the same vein, the former Soviet Union, East Europeans and Cuba, intervened in the Angolan civil war in favour of the MPLA because the FNLA and UNITA had American and South African support. It should be emphasized that during the whole period of superpower competition, their interventions in Africa's crisis was not necessarily to resolve the conflict nor to address the broader problems of the continent but rather to satisfy their narrow big power concerns. It should also come as no surprise that it was mainly the ruling African regimes that were the net beneficiaries. For as long as the Cold War bipolar international order persisted, the two major powers could be relied upon to automatically take sides in any major national or regional conflict in Africa. As was earlier pointed out, not infrequently the transferred arms were used by those ruling regimes to consolidate their power by suppressing their political rivals.

These broad conclusions respond, in a way, to our initial theoretical questions that were posed at the beginning of the discussion: whose peace and whose security ? and, what are the threats? It is also refreshing to note that superpowers often had no difficulty in supporting domestically unpopular and repressive regimes anywhere on the continent as long as those regimes served their strategic, economic and political interests well. At the same time, they would turn a blind eye on wanton repressions, mass poverty and all forms of underdevelopment. There is no doubt in our minds that the realist assumptions never envisaged international security alliances that supported domestic repressions. This is yet another important area where the received theory fails to encapsulate the security environment in the Third World. The end of the Cold War will hopefully put an end to the "double standards" syndrome of the big Western powers. They will be hard-pressed to stand on a high moral ground to vindicate their propaganda about democracy and human liberties that they were fond of parading against their communist foes in the past.

Moreover, the structurally fragile and weak states in the Third World in general and Africa in particular offered superpowers irresistible opportunities not only to test each other's nerves, but most importantly, to sell and test the effectiveness of their weapon systems. The efficiency of their hardware and intelligence capabilities were thus tested on the Third World soil and people. Tandon (1992: 27-28) correctly concluded that "the Third World life and limb had become dispensable in the interest of the Cold War contenders." Earlier Gupta (1978:134) had so eloquently captured this argument when he said that:

the very stability of the global power balance and the determination of the great powers to avoid a confrontation (which) makes them prone to seek lower levels of conflict and less dangerous ways of conducting their rivalries, which, in effect, means a concerted effort to confine their conflicts to problems that impinge on them less directly and to localize them in such area as far removed from the areas where their vital interests are involved. To fight out their battles in the Third World is one way of ensuring that their own worlds are not touched by their conflicts and that they retain a great measure of option to escalate and de-escalate their conflicts according to the needs of their relationships.

It is against this background that some attempts are now being made to recast the Third World national security problematique. In our view, national security in Africa should be explained as a product of a dynamic interaction between the internal and external threats. Much as the external security environment is very important, it does not necessarily determine or dictate the complex nature of Africa's security issues. Domestic factors such as the underdeveloped economies, narrowly based legitimacy, loose social integration, weak policy capacity and the lack of democracy, play equally important roles in shaping the national security posture. Finally, security and peace studies in the African context should be situated in a historical context. In our view, it is a useless intellectual exercise simply to count guns, warships and the frequency and geographic scope of armed conflicts in order to determine the degree of aggressiveness between great powers and minor states in the world system of states. The basic concern should be to understand the causes for those wars so as to seek for the solution. In this regard, it is impossible to explain today's Africa boundary disputes, the irredentist movements and ethnic rivalries without a clear understanding of the arbitrary creation of those nation-states, the legacy of divide-and-rule and the fragmentation of societies without an appreciation of its colonial past. In the same vein, direct emulation and the adoption of Western national security management tools and techniques is surely unwise. It is proposed that more imaginative techniques be sought that will be context specific, taking into account the nature and sources of the threats, the resources available, and possible peace alternatives at the disposal.

4. Peace and Security in Southern Africa: Problems and Prospects

In the wake of post-cold war, students of international relations are compelled to recast their theoretical frameworks to explain new patterns of global peace and security. As already noted, at the height of East-West conflict, the superpower perceptions of each other took on the image of the world that was divided between the forces of good and those of evil. Their mutual suspicions and rivalries drove them into the internal political affairs of the Third World. Lately, however, with the disintegration of the Soviet Union as a superpower, the global political terrain has been transformed and so should our perspectives. Together with the end of the cold war, the Southern African sub-region has just witnessed the end of the decolonization process as well as the halt in the destabilization campaigns by regional leviathan. Whatever the negotiations outcome of the South African, Mozambican, and Angolan conflicts, new security concerns that were either previously suppressed or those arising from the resolution of the current set of conflicts, will come to the fore. It is argued in this paper that the security concerns that are likely to emerge in the region, other than the continued foreign economic domination and dependence and political manipulations, will reflect the overriding contradictions rooted in their colonial histories hitherto camouflaged by the din and dust of the superpower competition and interventions.

As was earlier observed, a significant part of the conceptualization of regional security revolved around those external threats to the sub-system. Whether the context was that of the communist threat to western interests, the communist onslaught on South Africa, or the imperialist threat to the national liberation struggles, the debate on foreign intervention and evolvement set the security agenda for the region (Geldenhuys 1982; Nolutshungu, 1985). During that whole period, national and regional alliances pursued a combination of vague and often-times contradictory approaches. In one breath, most of the states in the region requested for arms from the Soviet bloc and/or China to help liberation movements. In the second breath, the same states solicited for Western economic assistance. In the third breath, they supported the Western and the UN mediation efforts in Zimbabwe, Angola and Namibia. This pattern of political behaviour manifestly confirm the proposition made that indeed, weak and fragile socio-political structures are highly vulnerable to external powers and pressures.

With the collapse of both the bi-polar power arrangement and ideological rivalry, the end of the decolonization process and the imminent transfer of power in South Africa, the security concerns in the region are bound to take on a radically different course. As Buzan (1991:435) has insightfully pointed out, a multi-centred core without contradictory ideologies means both a reduction in the intensity of global political concerns and a reduction in the resources available for sustained interventions. In other words, the value of the periphery countries as either ideological spoils or strategic assets in the great power rivalry has been dramatically reduced by the recent world development. The emerging Western indifference to the civil wars in the Sudan, Liberia and Ethiopia portends, to great measure, a kind of a new relationship between great powers and regional security systems in the Third World. This in turn, points to the rise of regional power politics in the periphery countries with the least possible big power interventions. Ayoob (1992:282) tends to concur with Buzan's observation and adds that:

> But were the superpowers to pull back, it might lead to greater assertiveness on the part of regionally pre-eminent powers interested in translating their pre-eminence into hegemony or at least into a managerial role within their respective regions.

Relatedly, Buzan makes yet another argument that "the outcome of domestic and even regional rivalries within the periphery should, other things being equal, be of less interest to the great powers than previously" (1991:442). Even in pure economic terms, Falk (1992:132) has suggested that, after all, those raw materials that were previously ranked as "strategic" (i.e industrial diamond, chrome, platinum and uranium from Southern Africa) in the East-West calculations, can now be easily procured from the former Soviet Union. As for most agricultural raw materials, biotechnology is already swiftly eroding the traditional Third World comparative advantage in tropical agricultural crops. Africa's key cash crops like sugar, cocoa, cotton and timber already have their biotechnology engineered substitutes in Europe (Clark and Juma, 1991).

There is also a growing public feeling in government circles in Africa that the West is gradually getting disinterested in the African countries. The arguments range from donor fatigue, heavy debt burdens to corrupt and inefficient governments. The focus seems to be on the former Soviet bloc countries. The Western concern about Eastern Europe will naturally take precedence over the Third World since it is clearly one of the European Community priority interests to have stable rather than unstable neighbours (Ohlson and Stedman, 1991). If it so transpires, the consequences are likely to be less and less external aid, investments and technology flowing to this continent. These observations should, however, be taken with some caution. In specific situations where the economic interests of great powers will be threatened by belligerent actions of some periphery states, military interventions should not be ruled out. The recent Gulf War demonstrates the Western concern for strategic resources like "their oil supplies" in the Middle East. This means, therefore, that the political space of the would-be "regional sub-imperialists" will also be highly circumscribed.

Other related recent events in the sub-region have demonstrated the United States deep continuing concern for the unfolding political processes in Southern Africa. In collaboration with the government of Botswana, the US is upgrading the latter's air defence capability by funding the construction of three airbase sites to the tune of US$1 billion and training her airforce. The airbases are scheduled for completion in 1993. The government of Botswana intends to cover the costs of construction by leasing them to the US Airforce and other US agencies. The main site is 35 kilometres northwest of the city of Gaborone; another one at Chobe near the border with Zambia and Zimbabwe; and, the third is near Okavango delta and the border with Namibia's Caprivi Strip separating Botswana and Angola. Above all, a recent joint US-Botswana military field exercise in Gaborone in 1991 confirms the latest superpower interest in the region (*Africa Confidential*, 1992:4-5). Military alliances between a big power and an African state naturally causes a lot of anxiety to the neighbours. Undoubtedly this incidence should have raised security concern in the sub-region. In the following section, we sketch out in a skeleton form what we consider to be some of the major conflict-prone issue areas in the region for the twenty first century.

4.1 Political Sources of Insecurity

The dominant factors that have produced conflict and insecurity in Southern Africa have been settler colonialism and the South African system of Apartheid and its brutal campaigns to dominate the surrounding black majority ruled states. The collapse of the white minority rule in South Africa will most likely leave behind it, arguably, a very precarious insecurity environment. To be sure, conflict and perceptions of insecurity do constitute serious obstacles to socio-economic development and inter-state cooperation. At nation and regional levels, we envisage the following conflict issues to emerge and occupy a security centre stage in the region in the 1990s and beyond.

1)   Legitimacy Crisis: conflicts over the control of the state and its institutions in the wake of political pluralism are likely to engender insecurity pressures in the region. Here we are interested in studying the capacity of states in the region to develop, nurture and sustain broad-based democracy, democratic institutions and practices amidst thriving civil societies and political parties.

2)   The Crisis of settling demobilized armed soldiers: conflicts associated with war termination, emergence of warlords *a la* Somalia leading towards almost uncontrollable downward spiral of insecurity, mass violence and misery (Patel, 1992:14-19). Here we are interested in examining case studies of potential "state failure" in Mozambique, Angola and South Africa should settlement negotiations fail.

3)   Border conflicts: contestations over colonially demarcated boundaries and their inherent potential of giving rise to armed confrontations and/or attempts either to secede or irredent. Countries to be studied are: South Africa, should whites and some homelands decide to secede; Tanzania and Zanzibar on the issue of the union; Tanzania and Malawi over the Lake Nyasa/Malawi border; Namibia and South Africa over the Walvis Bay question; and, Namibia and Botswana over the Sidudu Island.

4)   Foreign interventions particularly the UN from the Botswana airbases for regional pacification. Here we shall be trying to study the vicious circle of insecurity in the region as foreign powers intervene to restore peace and security. Questions to be addressed are the collapse of state structures in some countries; refugees problem; environmental degradation; and starvation and mass violence.

5)   Conflict over identity due to ethnicity, race, class and religious affiliations. The spillovers from economic inequality based on race; religious intolerance and fundamentalism; political marginalization of some groups are all likely to set in motion instability in different countries of the region.

6)   Reassertion of South Africa as a regional hegemon and impose *Pax Pretoriana* on the entire region (Vale, 1992). This would put an end to all anticipated efforts towards a collective security system and regional integration efforts. Studies in this area will examine possible negotiation scenarios in South Africa that would warrant such outcome and propose tentative coping strategies for the region.

7)   Conflict over Confidence-Building Measures: after so many years of hostilities, suspicions and distrust in the region, some confidence-

building measures would be required. Problems of "military transparency" are likely to trigger suspicions and insecurity in the region. Issues to be studied in this area would include, among others: force levels; quality and quantity of military arsenals; military descaling programmes including force levels, budgets and new procurement; exchange of information on troop location and movements; and, joint military training and manoeuvres (Vieira and Ohlson, 1990).

8) Because of the ineffectiveness of the OAU Mediation Commitee and because interventions by African actors have been not only of an *ad hoc* nature but also had limited success, states in the region would be required to yield some sovereign prerogatives to a larger regional body for preventive diplomacy, peacemaking, peace-keeping and peace-building (Boutros Boutros-Ghali, 1992). The details of a regional security regime and their misinterpretation by member states would endanger rather than promote security. Studies in this issue area will focus on the historical experiences of other regional groupings to isolate sensitive areas of misinterpretation and target them for future policy discussions.

4.2 Economic Sources of Insecurity

Economic development is one of the universal *sine qua non* conditions for peace and security. A state that does not have the capacity to provide for its people the basic necessities of life . . . food, shelter and clothing . . . is essentially insecure. The following set of issues are candidate economic sources of insecurity in Southern Africa.

1) Iniquitous Ownership and Development Patterns: unequal access to resources and regional inequalities are potential threats to peace and security. Deprivation of land in the former settler colonies of Zimbabwe, Namibia and South Africa constitutes a gross violation of basic human rights. As Makamure (1992) aptly argued, "reserves (add homelands) are nothing but large scale refugee camps resulting from white expropriation of land and country". Specific studies in this issue area have to examine how respective states are handling the land question within the peace and security problematique.

2) Economic Stagnation and Insecurity. Since the late 1970s, the Southern African region has been characterized by economic stagnation, worsening terms of trade and growing indebtedness. That gloom economic picture was exacerbated by the devastating impact of Pretoria's policies of aggression and destabilization. The recent

imposition of Structural Adjustment Programmes by the multilateral financial institutions pose a real danger to regional peace and stability. Those imposed restructuring programmes tend to marginalize the masses of the people and enrich a few of those who are already rich. Studies in this area will examine what alternative reform policy measures can be taken at national and regional levels to consolidate "national economies" and mitigate possible political instability. In fact, "IMF coups" are not uncommon on the continent!

3) Regional Cooperation and Integration. All concerned parties in the region are busy searching for a formula that will facilitate closer regional cooperation and integration based on the principles of equity, interdependence and mutual benefit. That hope can, however, easily turn into its opposite. Should some states in the region, South Africa in particular, push for short-sighted liberalization and deregulation of trade, finance, investment and transport services (particularly for landlocked states), poralization will be the outcome and will inevitably give rise to insecurity problems in the region (Davies, 1993). Studies in this area should seek to examine existing imbalances and inequalities; and, subsequently, propose collective endeavour that will redress the said imbalances and identify common income generating activities for all states in the region (e.g increase value added of minerals produced in the region, boost the production and supply of scarce resources like water and hydro power etc).

4.3 The Indian Ocean and Instability in the Region

The Indian Ocean is the third largest ocean in the world. It is estimated to cover an area of about 75 million square kilometres. There are well over forty states that are generally referred to as littoral states of the Indian Ocean. Those states carry about a third of the world's population. Above all, the Ocean joins four continents namely Africa, Asia, Europe and Australia. For the last four decades, the Indian Ocean was transformed into a theatre of great power competition. Now that the Cold War is behind us, the region should seek to participate effectively in the demilitarization exercise of the Indian Ocean as well as establishing an anti-toxic waste dumping regime. However, both suggestions are likely to engender inter-state conflicts.

1) Several Indian Ocean littoral states in the sub-region are likely to offer, for a handsome fee, their ports, deserts and airports as bases or simply calling stations for some extra-regional big powers. Such actions are likely to jeopardize any regional security arrangements that might be agreed upon and give rise to new forms of insecurity.

2)   It has been recently realized that some environmental issues like mass production of greenhouse gases or chemicals that erode the protective ozone layer or polluting activities threaten to overwhelm the conditions of human existence on a large scale (Deudney, 1990). The Indian Ocean is an easy target for toxic dumping from the West.

In both cases, studies will focus their attention on identifying critical factors in a regional security regime that are likely to erode stability from the environment point of view and suggest collective measures to arrest them.

In the final section of the paper, an attempt is made to present three hypothetical scenarios of possible national and regional security postures in the coming years. In all the three scenarios, the international system is taken as the independent variable. These scenarios are: the minimal levels of cooperation schemes based on the prevailing economic and political structures scenario; the emergence of South Africa as a bullish regional power scenario; and, the creation of a comprehensive collective regional economic and security arrangement embracing South Africa as a benevolent leader.

A minimalist approach proceeds from the assumptions that the West will have the least interest in the region and that its participation will be invariably indirect in most key aspects (except of course in economic affairs). Secondly, it is assumed that in the short and medium terms, all the states in the region will be embroiled in insecurity environments whose root causes are primarily historical in nature. The security issues likely to come to the centre stage are the security threats that will be unleashed by political transitions to multi-party rule and majority rule in South Africa with their attendant political openness; ethnic nationalism and border liquidations; the impact of economic crisis in the wake of insufficient external aid and diminished export receipts with the IMF and the World Bank imposing draconian measures to redress them and, most importantly, in order to collect Western debts; the legitimacy crisis of states resulting from unfair political play which, given the circumstances, the state will fail to exercise the ideological, political and intellectual leadership; and, the rise of the many historically suppressed nationalisms.

Under this nightmare scenario, therefore, the national security posture in all of these countries will be that of political decay characterized by mass riots, civil wars, refugee problems, ethnic nationalism and the break down of the economic and nation-state systems as presently constituted. National security in each nation-state will increasingly degenerate into regime insecurity characterised by indiscriminate state repressions leading to anarchy *a la* Somalia in several countries. Zaire, Mozambique, South Africa and Angola seem to be imminent candidates in our estimation. In these four countries a good percentage of the population has already been internally and externally displaced. They live in marginal areas in the countryside or in huge squatter camps on the edge of big towns. Following the formal end of political hostilities the demobilized troops and rebels are likely not to surrender their weapons for quite some time. These developments, in turn, will reduce the impetus towards maximal approaches to regional economic and political cooperation and integration. In the long run, the unexpected obverse might also come true. In addition to the political decay, the violence in this part of the world might be an integral part of the process of accumulation of power by the emerging national state apparatus. From the ruins of domestic struggles, political consensus may finally emerge in some countries as the major players would agree on the otherwise contentious issues. They would make hard choices, think much more clearly on how to put an end on their divided, fragmented loyalties and devise commonly accepted rules and political procedures and viable nation-states.[9] After examining political processes of the sixteenth and seventeenth century Europe, Huntington (1968:123) came to a similar conclusion that "war was the great stimulus to state building."

The second scenario is the consolidation of the Republic of South Africa as a bullish regional hegemony. Just as in the first scenario, it assumes that big powers will pay little attention to distant regional security configurations. In this scenario, minimum levels of regional security alliance, and economic cooperation and integration are envisaged under the South African hegemony. Moreover, precisely because of the structure of most economies in the region, South Africa is likely to dominate all member states in investment, trade and services. Finally, just like any hegemony in history, South Africa will monopolize the right to interpret the agreed norms, rules, and procedures of the regional security and economic arrangements. It is likely also to use its enormous power to impose the local solutions it prefers and veto those it dislikes in a kind of *"Pax Pretoriana"*.

As is well known, the Republic of South Africa has developed considerably formidable military capabilities and an elaborate economic and technological infrastructure. In international politics, one way that states have attempted to distinguish themselves from others is by increasingly modernizing their armies and by being perceived by others as having the willingness to use that capability to achieve its objectives. In this sense, South Africa will exploit its military capability to reap significant political and economic benefits as well as prestige in the region and beyond. "The ability to act" writes Kenneth Waltz (1983:640) "carries with it a temptation to take action". Under this scenario, the national security posture in the region will be that of constant uncertainty; the regional leviathan will arrogate itself the sole monopoly of interpreting the security regime to suit its immediate interests; it will militarily move in member nation-states allegedly to punish recalcitrant regimes or groups for one thing or another as impudently as it used to do under the apartheid regime. Much as the frequency of punitive military incursions in the neighbouring states by the regional hegemon might be rare, but the unequal distribution of the economic gains and asymmetrical regional security management arrangement will minimize rather than maximize the security concerns in the sub-region. For the type of peace that is likely to emerge from this scenario is one whereby stability exists as a product of foreign domination, coercion and subordination.

The last scenario falls between the first two. Our prognosis for the 1990s is not all gloom and doom. It is the least likely, but the most favoured. It envisages a formation of a comprehensive regional security based on cooperative principles and is development-orientated with South Africa behaving as a benevolent hegemony. To this proposition Ncube (1992:36) hastened to add that "the new regional relations should be based on cooperative principles . . . principles which assume that there is no self-appointed regional power". This position is also shared by the two leading national liberation movements namely the ANC and the PAC. History has ample evidence to demonstrate that, in fact, small states offset their weaknesses by forming alliances with others. Some observers have proposed the formation of a "Conference for Security and Cooperation in Southern Africa (CSDSA) along the model of the Conference for Security and Cooperation in Europe (CSCE). The CSCE, also known as the Helsinki process, provided a forum for the USA, the former Soviet Union and 33 West and East European countries to formulate guidelines on inter-state relations on security, economic cooperation and human rights. Its performance record, of course not forgetting the role of nuclear weapons, was rated as excellent (Bruce, 1991; Evera, 1991).

The proposed CSDSA is a brain-child of the African Leadership Forum. The tasks of the Conference would be to constitute an inter-state security arrangement that could promote institutionalized non-violent forms of conflict resolution; oversee and guarantee an end to external involvement in domestic and regional conflicts; facilitate the reduction in military expenditures; switch to non-offensive defence and generally perform the task of confidence building and regional identity (Mills and Clapham, 1991; Kampala Document, 1991). Economically, the Conference would be called upon to harmonize economic policies and strategies in the sub-region.

This scenario raises three bones of contention. First, a collective defence arrangement presupposes a collective overarching of historical animosities that need to be contained within permanent and structured conflict management mechanisms. This would include the establishment of joint military bodies, programmes, exchange of military information and intelligence (Ching'ambo, 1992). As earlier noted, in the unfolding political climate in the sub-region, the sense of a common regional enemy commanding a regional attention seems absent. The second tricky problem inherent in a collective security arrangement is identifying and agreeing on the collective enemy. Maull (1992: 5-6) has suggested that one way of going around this problem would be to follow certain pre-established rules of conduct such as the renunciation of force, submission to compulsory mediation, acceptance of peace keeping force and the like. Failure to comply with these procedures would be seen as identifying the enemy. The last problem with a regional security arrangement is a tendency by some alliance members to pursue parallel national and bilateral arrangements. The current arrangement between Botswana and the USA point to this direction. It has a potential to threaten a collective regional alliance arrangement that this scenario is proposing.

5. Conclusion

None of the three scenarios provided seem to promise any bright prospects for sustainable peace and security in the sub-region. In the short and medium runs, at least, one can envisage some limited peace dividends from the ending of East-West conflict. The warring factions in Mozambique and Angola have agreed to the ceasefire and to expeditiously negotiate the modalities of national reconciliation and reconstruction. The Convention for Democratic South Africa (CODESA) though fraught with the initial negotiation complexities, the ball has begun rolling. Elsewhere in the sub-region, the democratization processes are well on course. The intriguing question is what political outcome are we likely to witness? As already noted, anything is possible, ranging from the disintegration of the current nation-states, the formation of more viable states to the creation of a formidable regional economic and security bloc. The final outcome will largely depend on how the current conflicts are handled and resolved.

However, the size and magnitude of the crisis that is engulfing the continent is both economic and political. This crisis is manifested in the abysmal declines in economic indicators and trends as well as in the impoverishment of the vast majority of people. On the political terrain, there has been pervasive monopolization of power by tiny political elites in each country. As was argued, the lack of effective participation was generally found to be one of the major causes of social unrest and political insecurity. It is therefore recommended that all nation-states in the sub-region individually and collectively create institutional structures and design policies and programmes that serve the interests of all sections in society. At the same time, political processes should be opened up to accommodate freedom of opinions, tolerate differences, accept consensus on issues and ensure effective participation of people and their associations and organizations. A conscious promotion of popular participation of the citizens as individuals or as associations would definitely drastically reduce the incidence of political alienation and revolt.

The uneven and unequal development in each nation-state has resulted, among other things, in different social cleavages developing fragmented loyalties and seeking solutions to their problems through unorthodox channels. In this regard we are suggesting that future development policies, strategies and programmes be in line with the interests and aspirations of the people, and that they should be culturally and socially compatible with the prevailing realities. Development in this sense should seek to strengthen national sovereignty, create a self-reliant and self-sustaining economy, improve the social and political environment of the citizens and enhance the cultural cohesion of society, integrity and dignity of everyone in the nation.

One can also safely conclude that precisely because states will be politically accountable, threats to the state, particularly those arising from abroad, will be freely debated and the action taken will have broad popular support. Misguided political adventurism will be as much as possible avoided. In the same vein, all states are encouraged to use similar democratic processes to establish the structures and procedures necessary for collective security and development. There are several security concerns in the region that would call for collective action. These would include among others, descaling national security forces to acceptable levels; the demilitarization of the Indian Ocean; enforcement of the international Law of the Sea; and, collective campaigns against ocean pollution. The demilitarization proposals for the Indian Ocean have been around with us for quite some time now (Shephard, 1985). Now that the

Cold war is behind us, collaborative efforts should be directed towards the demilitarization of the Indian Ocean as well as enforcing the Law of the Sea particularly as regards the protection and exploitation of the Ocean resources.

Footnotes

* This research paper was prepared for the Southern Africa Political Economy Series (SAPES) Trust when the author was a Visiting Research Fellow at the SAPES Trust, in June 1993, Harare, Zimbabwe.

1. Students of peace research have considerably expounded on and enriched the meaning of the concept "peace" to mean not only the absence of direct physical violence but also the presence of reasonable levels of individual and societal well-being necessary to facilitate the fulfilment of the basic needs as well as some normative values such as integrity, dignity, identity and much else. For insightful discussions on the subject, see Galtung, J. (1969:167-191) and Wallensteen, P. (1988).

2. The paradigm of global security refers to a system of global order or system. As Bloch (1959) aptly concluded, a system which presupposes a universal concept of security with a shared set of norms, principles and practices which result in common patterns of international behaviour is a utopia but theoretically possible.

3. The realist theorists agree that the state is the prime actor in international political life, that force is widely available and frequently used to adjust relations on the bases of power, and that humanist values offer neither the guide for action nor a basis for appraisal. For modern realist classics see Carr, 1939; and, Morgenthau, 1948.

4. Keohane (1980:33) defined a security regime as a regularized cooperative behaviour in issues relating to the national security of two or more states, governed by either explicit or implicit norms and rules which permit nations to be restrained in their behaviour in the belief that others will reciprocate.

5. The Kampala Document, for example, defines security as "all aspects of society including economic, political and social dimension of individual, family, community, local and national life . . . .. Lack of democracy in which people freely participate in government, denial of personal liberties, abuse of religion, precedence given to military expenditures over other sectors of national life, and the lack of proper administrative machinery for the control and management of public funds are some of the deep-rooted causes of insecurity", p. 23.

6. Barry Buzan (1983 132-134) has neatly defined "weak states" not in a military sense, but weak because they are new, inexperienced and/or lack effective control over their population, and particularly over national minorities.

7. The slicing of the African continent into numerous small and heterogeneous nation-states is often compared to the partition of south eastern Europe in the 19th and 20th centuries out of the Ottoman Empire. A discussion of this comparison can be found in Mazrui and Tidy (1984:66-67).

8. Article III of the OAU Charter calls on all member states to deny operation of military bases by any extra-regional powers. However, a dozen or so African countries have entered into security alliances with big powers who are guaranteed base facilities. For a perceptive analysis on this issue see Arlinghaus, B. (1983).

9. There is a general tolerance of secessionist movements in the current political thinking in the global community as demonstrated by the recognition of Armenia, Croatia, Estonia and Eritrea, Katanga, Zanzibar and Kwazulu are likely to follow suit.

References

Africa Confidential, Feb. 7, 1992,"Where the Eagles Fly" Vol. 33, No.3 pp. 3-4.

Ajala, A., 1983, "The Nature of African Boundaries" *Afrika Spectrum* No. 83 pp.175-192.

Albright, D., 1973, "Moscow's African Policy of the 1970s" in *Communism in Africa*. (ed) Albright, D., Bloomington: Indiana University Press. pp.35-66.

Anyang' Nyongo, P., 1986, "An African Perspective on Peace and Development" in *International Social Science Journal* Vol. 38 No.4 pp.575-588.

Arlinghaus, B.,(ed).1984, *Africa Security Issues: Sovereignty, Stability and Solidarity*, Boulder: West View Press.

Arnold, M., 1991, "Africa in the 1990s" *The Fletcher Forum*, 1991.

Ayoob, M., 1991, "The Security Problematic of the Third World" *World Politics* Vol. 43 No.2 pp.257-283.

-----,1987, "The Roots of the Conflicts" in *Conflict and Intervention in the Third World*. (ed) M. Ayoob. New York: St. Martin's Press, pp.239-252.

Azar, E. and C. Moon (eds), 1988, *National Security in the Third World: The Management of Internal and External Threats*. Idershot: Edward Elga Publishing House.

Bloch, E.,1959, *Das Prinzip Hoffnung*, Frankfurt: Suhrkamp Verlag.

Bruce, G., 1991, "Negotiation on Confidence and Security Building Measures: The Vienna Agreement and Beyond" *NATO Review* Vol. 39 No. 1 pp. 15-20.

Buchan, A., 1966, *War in Modern Societies*, London: Collins.

Bull, H., (ed) 1984, *Intervention in World Politics*, Oxford: Clarendon.

Buzan, B., 1991, "New Patterns of Global Security in the Twenty First Century" in *International Affairs* Vol. 67 No. 3 pp.431- 452.

-----1983, *People, States and Fear*, Sussex: Harvester Press Ltd.

Carr, E., 1939, *The Twenty Years' Crisis 1919-1939*. New York: St. Martin's Press.

Curzon, K., *Frontiers*, London.

Davies, R. *et al*.1979, "Class Struggle and the Periodization of the State in South Africa" *Review of African Political Economy* No. 7 pp. 33-36.

-----1993, "Emerging South African Perspectives on Regional Cooperation and Integration After Apartheid" in *South Africa After Apartheid* (ed) B. Oden, Uppsala: Nordiska Afrikainstitutet, 1993 pp.71-86.

Deudney, D., 1990, "The Case Against Linking Environmental Degradation and National Security" *Millennium*, Vol. 19 No. 3 pp.461-476.

Donaldson, R.(ed), 1981, *The Soviet Union in the Third World: Success and Failures*. Boulder: West View Press.

Evera, S., 1991, "Primed for Peace: Europe After the Cold War" *International Security* Vol. 15 pp. 48-50.

Falk, R.,1992, "Recycling Interventionism" *Journal of Peace Research*. Vol. 29 No, 2 pp 129-134.

Galtung, J., 1967, "Violence, Peace and Peace Research" in *Journal of Peace Research* Vol. 6 pp.167-191.

Geldenhuys, D.,1982, "South Africa and the West" in R. Schrire (ed). *South Africa: Public Policy Perspectives*, Johannesburg: Juta and Co. pp.299-339.

Ghali, B., 1992, *An Agenda for Peace: Preventive Diplomacy, Peacemaking and Peace-keeping*, New York: UN.

Girvan, N., 1984, "Swallowing the IMF Medicine in the 1980s" in *Development Dialogue* No. 2 pp.54-74.

Goldsworth, D., 1980, "South Africa" in M. Ayoob (ed), *Conflict and Intervention in the Third World*, New York: St. Martins Press.pp. 205-238.

Grechkov, A., 1975, "The Leading Role of the CPSU in Building the Army of a Developed Socialist Society" *in Strategic Review* Vol. 3 No. 1 p.90.

Gupta S. 1978, "Great Power Relations, World Order and the Third World" in *Foreign Affairs Reports* Vol 27 No. 7-8.

Haftendorn, H., 1991, "The Security Puzzle: Theory Building and Discipline Building in International Security" *International Studies Quarterly* Vol. 35 No. 3 pp. 3-17.

Herbst, J., 1989 "The Creation and Maintenance of National Boundaries in Africa" *International Organization* Vol. 43 No. 4 pp.673-692.

Herz, J., 1950, "Idealist Internationalism and the Security Dilemma" *World Politics*, Vol. 2 No. 2 pp. 157-80.

Hjelm-Wallen, L., 1991, "The Spirit of San Francisco" *Society for Internation Development*, Vol. 3/4.

Hoffman, S., 1980, *Primacy or World Order?* New York: MacGraw-Hill.

Horowitz, 1981 "Patterns of Ethnic Separatism" *Comparative Studies in Society and History* Vol. 23 pp. 165-195.

Huntington, S., 1968, *Political Order in Changing Societies*, New Haven: Yale University Press.

Ibingira, G., 1980, *Africa Upheavals Since Independence*, Boulder: Westview Press.

Jackson, R., 1990, *Quasi-States and Sovereignty in Africa: International Relations and the Third World*. Cambridge: University of Cambridge Press.

Jackson, R. and C. Rosberg, 1983, *Personal Rule in Black Africa,* Berkeley, Los Angeles: University of California Press.

-----1982,"Why African Weak States Persist: The Empirical and the Juridical Statehood" *World Politics* Vol. 35 pp.1-24.

The Kampala Document, 1991, *Towards a Conference on Security, Stability, Development and Cooperation in Africa*, Kampala.

Kemp, G.,1977, *Arms Traffic and the Third World Conflict*, New York: Carnegie Endowment.

Keohane, R., 1980, "The Theory of Hegemonic Stability and Changes in International Economic Regimes 1967-1977" in *Change in the International System*, (eds) Holsti, O.; R. Siverson and A. George, Boulder, CO.: Westview Press, pp. 131-162.

Korany, B., 1986, "Strategic Studies and the Third World: A Critical Evaluation" *International Social Science Journal* Vol. 38 No. 4 pp.547-562.

Krause, L. and J. Nye, 1975, "Reflections on the Economics and Politics of International Economic Organizations" in Bengsten F.and L. Krause (eds) *World Politics and International Economics*. Washington DC.: Brookings Institution.

Lappmann, W.,1943, *US Foreign Policy: Shield of the Republic*, Boston: Little, Brown and Co.

Loxley, J., 1987, "The IMF, the World Bank and Sub-Saharan Africa: Policies and Politics" in Havnevik K. (ed), *The IMF and the World Bank in Africa*, Uppsala: Scandinavian Institute of African Studies, pp. 47-64.

MacFarlane, S.,1984, "Africa Decaying Security Systems and the Rise of Intervention" *International Security*, Vol. 8 No. 4 p.127-151.

Makamure, K. "The Land Debate in Zimbabwe: Laying the Parameters" in *SAPEM* Vol. 5 No.7 pp.9.

Mandaza, I., 1992. "The Frontline States: A Mission Revived" *SAPEM* Vol. 5 No. 7 pp.37-40.

-----1991, *Southern Africa in the 1990s: Towards a Research Agenda*, SAPES Occasional Paper Series No.1.

Mazrui, A. and M. Tidy, 1984, *Nationalism and the New States in Africa*, Exeter, New Hampshire: Heinemann Books.

Mills, G.and C. Clapham, 1991, *Southern African Security After Apartheid: A Framework for Analysis,* A Working Paper Series, Centre for Southern African Studies, University of Western Cape.

Morgenthau, H. and K. Thompson, 1956, *Principles and Problems of International Politics,* New York: Knopf.

Nathan, L., 1992, "Towards a Conference on Security, Stability, Development and Cooperation in Africa" *Africa Insight* Vol. 22 No. 3 pp.212-217.

Ncube, P. 1992,"Possible Future Relations in Southern Africa" *SAPEM* Vol. 5 No. 5 pp.35-36.

Nelson, H. *et al.,* 1975, *Area Handbook for Malawi*, Washington DC: US Government Printing Office.

Nolutshungu, S., 1985, "Soviet Involvement in South Africa" *Annals* No. 481 pp.138-146.

Nye, Jr. J. 1992 "Soft Power" *Foreign Affairs*, No. 8 pp.153-171.

Ohlson, T. and S. Stedman "Trick or Treat? The End of Bipolarity and Conflict Resolution in Southern Africa" *Southern African Perspectives* Working Paper No. 11, University of West Cape, pp. 10-11.

Osgood, R. 1982, *Containment: Soviet Behaviour and Grand Strategy*, Berkeley, California: Institute of International Studies.

Ottaway, M.,1982, *Soviet and American Influence in the Horn of Africa*, New York: Prager Publishers.

Patel. H., 1992 "Peace and Security in Changing Southern Africa: A Frontline View" *Southern African Perspectives*, University of West Cape, Working Paper No. 12.

Payer, C.,1974, *The Debt Trap: The IMF and the Debt Trap*, New York: Monthly Review.

Rodney, W., 1982, *How Europe Underdeveloped Africa*, Washington DC,: Howard University Press.

Rugumamu, S.,1991a "National Security Dilemma in Africa: Setting the Record Straight" *Tanzanian Journal of Development Studies*. Vol.1 No.1 pp.64-77.

-----1991b, "National Security in Africa: Problems of Analysis" in *SAPEM*, Vol. 5 No. 2 pp.51-52.

Sautter, G., 1982, "Quelques Reflexions sur Les Frontieres Africaines" in *Frontieres: Problemes de Frontieres dans le Tiere Monde*, Paris: Universite Paris. pp.35-49.

Seidman A. 1985, *The Roots of Crises in Southern Africa*, Trenton: N.J.: Africa World Press.

Separd, G., 1985, "Demilitarization Proposals for the Indian Ocean" in Bowman L. and I. Clark (eds), *The Indian Ocean in Global Politics*, Boulder: Westview Press. pp.223-247.

Tandon Y., "Impact of the Demise of the USSR on the Third World" *SAPEM* Vol. 5 No. 9 pp.25-31.

Terabrin, E.,1983, "Ekspansconistskaia Politika SSHAV Afrike" in *Mezhduna Rodnaia Zhizn*, No. 9 pp. 46-47.

Tillema, H., 1988, "Foreign Overt Military Intervention in the Nuclear Age" *Journal of Peace Research*, Vol. 26 No.2 pp.179-196.

Trager, F. and P. Kronenberg (ed), 1973, *National Security and American Society: Theories, Processes and Policy*, Lawrence: Kansas, University of Kansas Press.

UNICEF, 1989, *Children on the Frontline: The Impact of Apartheid, Destabilization, and Warfare on Children in Southern and South Africa*, New York: UNICEF.

Vale, P., 1992, *Hoping Against Hope: The Prospects for South Africa's Post-Apartheid Regional Policy*, SAPES Mimeo.

Verobyev, V., 1978, "Colonialist Policies in Africa" in *International Affairs*, No. 9 pp. 47-49.

Vieira, S. and T. Ohlson, 1990, *Arms Transfer Limitations and the Relationship with Peace, Security and Development*, SAPES Mimeo.

Walfers, A., 1962, *Discord and Collaboration: Essays in International Politics*, Baltimore: Johns Hopkins University Press.

Wallensteen, P. 1988, "Understanding Conflict Resolution: A Framework" in Wallensteen P., *Peace Research: Achievements and Challenges*, Boulder: Westview Press.

Waltz, K. 1983 "A strategy for Rapid Deployment Force" in Art, R.and K Waltz (eds), *The Use of Force: International Politics and Foreign Policy*, Lanham, MD. : University Press of America.

-----1979, *The Theory of International Politics*, Reading: Mass.: Addison-Wesley.

Zartman, W. 1966, *International Relations in New Africa*, Englewood Cliffs, N.J.: Prentice-Hall.